LOOK INSIDE

Telephone

Catherine Chambers

Heinemann Interactive Library
Des Plaines, Illinois

© 1998 Reed Educational & Professional Publishing
Published by Heinemann Interactive Library,
an imprint of Reed Educational & Professional Publishing,
1350 East Touhy Avenue, Suite 240 West
Des Plaines, IL 60018

Designed by Celia Floyd
Printed in Hong Kong

02 01 00 99 98
10 9 8 7 6 5 4 3 2 1

Library of Congress Cataloging-in-Publication Data
Chambers, Catherine, 1954-
        Telephone / Catherine Chambers.
            p.   cm. — (Look inside)
        Includes bibliographical references and index.
        Summary: A brief introduction to the telephone, how it is
    constructed, and how to use it.
        ISBN 1-57572-625-4 (lib. bdg.)
        1. Telephone—Juvenile literature.   [1. Telephone.]   I. Title.
    II. Series: Chambers, Catherine, 1954-   Look inside.
    TK6165.C48   1998
    621.386—dc21   97-31457
                                                                        CIP
                                                                        AC

Acknowledgments
The publisher would like to thank the following for permission to reproduce photographs: Chris Honeywell, pp. 4–21

Cover photograph: Chris Honeywell

Our thanks to Betty Root for her comments in the preparation of this book and to Geemark Telecom Ltd for their assistance.

Every effort has been made to contact copyright holders of any material reproduced in this book. Any omissions will be rectified in subsequent printings if notice is given to the publisher.

Some words are shown in bold, **like this**. You can find out what they mean by looking in the glossary.

CONTENTS

HERE'S A TELEPHONE

All these bits and pieces make up a
telephone. The small parts make the
telephone work.
They fit inside
the large,
smooth shell.

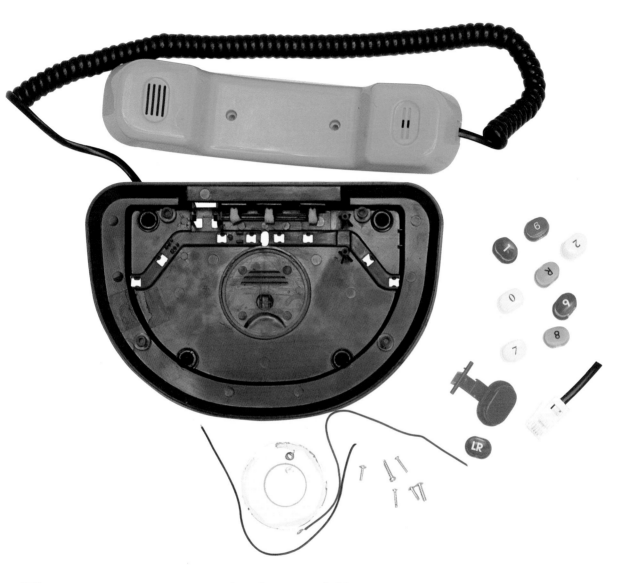

The pieces are made from different materials. You can see hard metal parts and **flexible** metal wires. There is tough, shiny plastic and thin, **fragile** plastic.

THE DIALING UNIT

The dialing **unit** is made from two pieces. The bottom piece is flat. It covers the small electronic pieces. There are spaces for each working part. Buttons and wires are working parts.

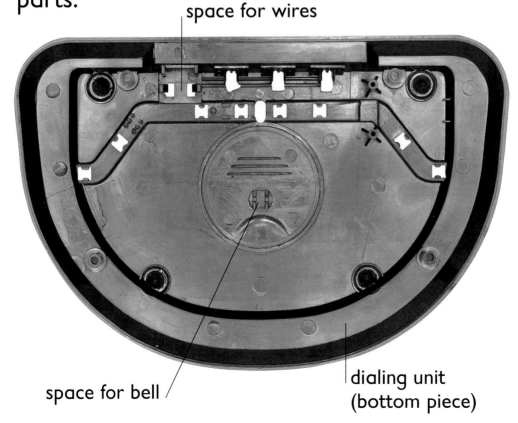

space for wires

space for bell

dialing unit
(bottom piece)

One part of the top piece is curved. This is where the receiver fits. Below this are holes for the buttons. Both parts of the unit are made from tough plastic.

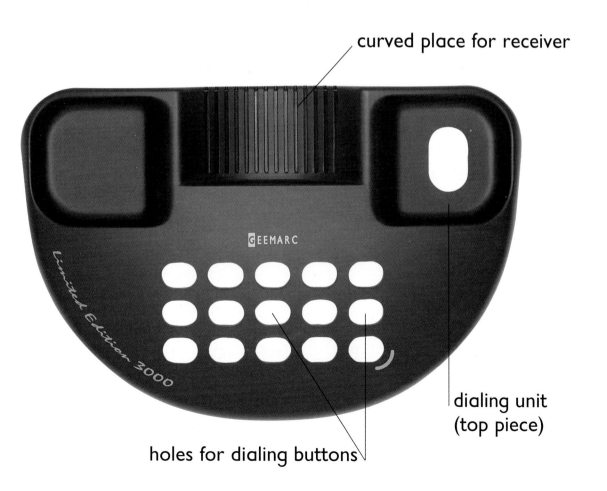

curved place for receiver

GEEMARC

Limited Edition 3000

dialing unit
(top piece)

holes for dialing buttons

DIALING A NUMBER

receiver button

dialing buttons

GEEMARC

Limited Edition 3000

The buttons are made from tough plastic. They are close together. This makes dialing phone numbers easy. Each button sits on a soft spring. This makes the buttons easy to push.

wires from buttons go into telephone

Each button has a number, letter, or symbol on it. When you press a button, an **electric signal** travels through wires. The signal opens a clear line to another telephone and makes the other telephone ring.

"RING-RING!"

The ringing sound is made inside the telephone. An **electric signal vibrates** against a thin plastic disk. This disk is called a diaphragm. The diaphragm vibrates, too. It moves the air around it, making waves of ringing sound.

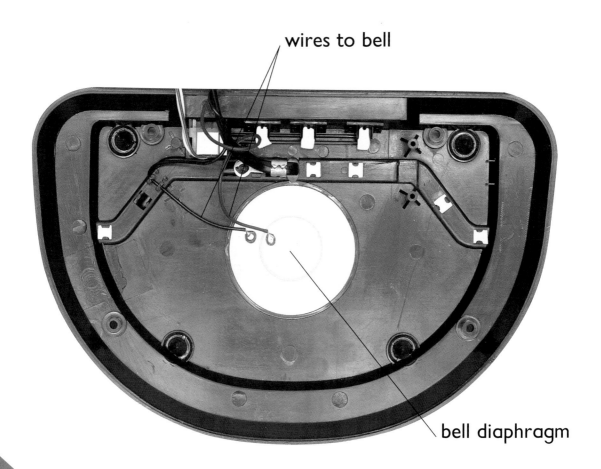

wires to bell

bell diaphragm

The receiver rests on a button. This button connects the electric signal to the diaphragm. When you pick up the receiver, the button springs up. The electric connection is broken and the phone stops ringing.

button is pressed

connection is made

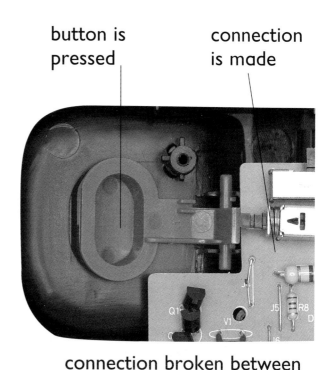

connection broken between receiver button and bell

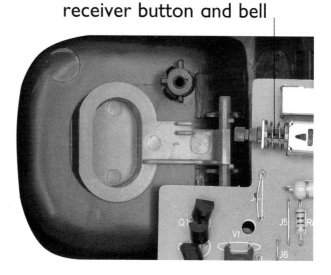

THE RECEIVER

The receiver is made up of two parts. They are curved to fit around the side of your face. The mouthpiece and earpiece curve inwards. They are close to your mouth and your ear.

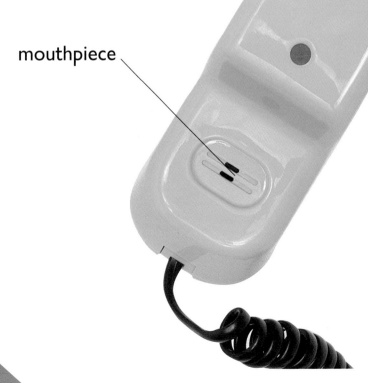

earpiece

mouthpiece

Both pieces are made of tough plastic. One piece is a cover. It clips onto the part with the electronic parts, the mouthpiece, and earpiece. These have holes in them. This is so you can speak and listen.

inside the receiver

cover of receiver

SPEAKING

Your voice is really waves of sound that move through air. A microphone inside the mouthpiece turns your voice into **electric signals**. The microphone has a very thin disk. Your voice makes this disk **vibrate**.

microphone

The disk presses against tiny bits of **carbon** packed into a **cylinder**. An electric current flows through the bits. The **pressure** turns these into electric signals. The signals then travel along the wires.

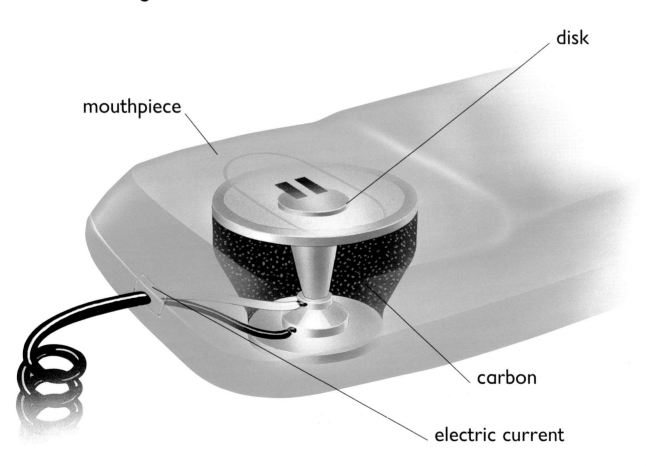

disk

mouthpiece

carbon

electric current

WIRES

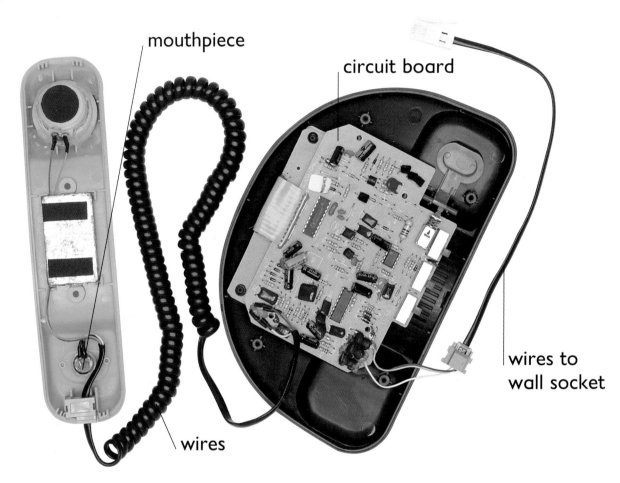

mouthpiece

circuit board

wires to wall socket

wires

Copper wires run from the receiver into the dialing unit. They pass along a **circuit board** and out to a wall **socket**. The wires are covered with colored plastic. They go from your house into the ground or to telephone poles.

Underground wires are often made of two glass tubes called optical fibers. One tube is inside the other. The tubes carry the sound of your voice as light signals instead of **electric signals**. These bounce along the glass until they reach the earpiece.

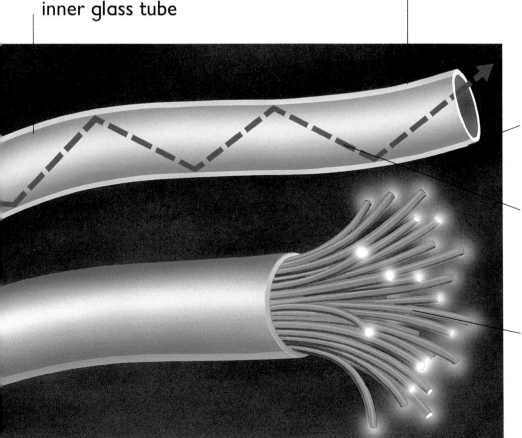

inner glass tube

a single optical fiber

outer glass tube

light signals bouncing along

a bundle of single optical fibers

THE EARPIECE

Wires run through the receiver. They carry **electric signals** to the earpiece. The electronic parts of the earpiece are inside a **cylinder**. Here, the electric signals move a tight wire **coil**. This is an electromagnet.

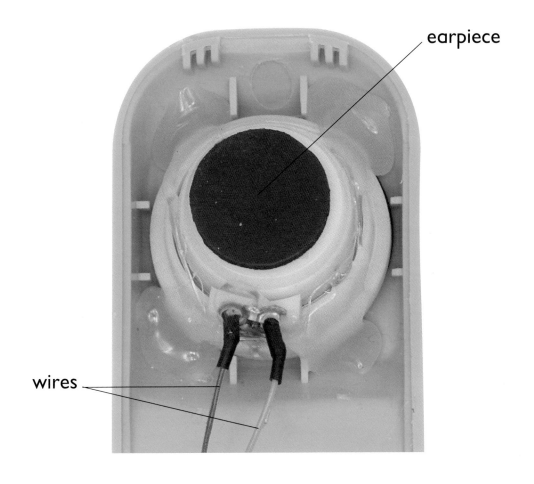

earpiece

wires

The electromagnet **vibrates** against a thin disk. The disk vibrates and makes sound waves in the air. Now you can hear the voice!

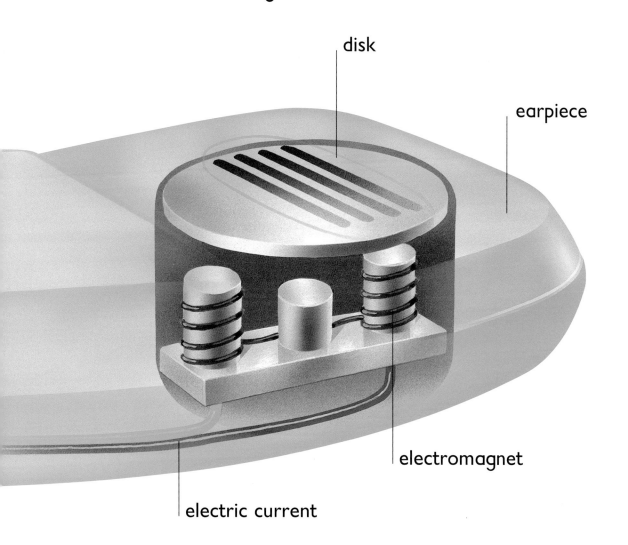

disk

earpiece

electromagnet

electric current

19

USING A TELEPHONE

Here is the telephone. It can fit on a desk. It can go on a wall. The receiver has a curly, stretchy cord. Some telephones have no wires or cords at all. You can take them anywhere.

The telephone is ringing. You can pick up the receiver and hold it easily. It weighs very little. This telephone is bright and colorful. Its shape is smooth, curved, and fun. Enjoy using it to talk with a friend!

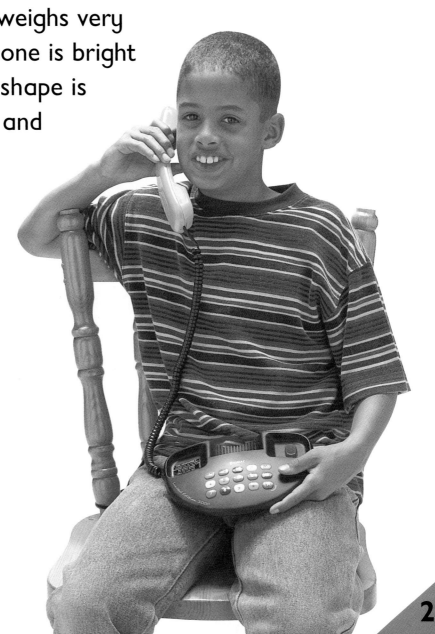

GLOSSARY

carbon important kind of material found in many things

circuit board board with tiny switches and wires that controls the flow of signals from one part of a machine to another

coil something that is twisted round and round, such as a spring

cylinder something that is shaped like a tube

electric signal message produced by electricity

flexible bends easily

fragile breaks easily

pressure force of something pressing down

socket hole made for a plug

unit single working machine

vibrates moves backwards and forwards very quickly

MORE BOOKS TO READ

Bendick, Jeanne. *Eureka! It's a Telephone!* Brookfield, Conn: Millbrook Press, 1993.

Stone, Amy. *Telephone.* Tarrytown, NY: Marshall Cavendish, 1995.

Weiss, Ellen. *Telephone Time: A First Book of Telephone Do's & Don'ts.* New York: Random Books For Young Readers, 1986.

INDEX